ABOVE & BEYOND

ABOVE & BEYOND

ABOVE OUR UNDERSTANDING
ABOVE OUR EXPECTATIONS

GARRY SHEAFFER

μ65

Powered by eGenCo   Generation Culture Transformation
Specializing in publishing for generation culture change

eGenCo
824 Tallow Hill Road
Chambersburg, PA 17202, USA
Phone: 717-461-3436
Email: info@micro65.com
Website: www.micro65.com

 facebook.com/egenbooks

 youtube.com/egenpub

 egen.co/blog

 pinterest.com/eGenDMP

 twitter.com/eGenDMP

 instagram.com/egenco_dmp

Publisher's Cataloging-in-Publication Data
Sheaffer, Garry
Above and Beyond. Above Our Understanding Beyond Our Expectation.;
by Garry Sheaffer. Rebekah Helman, editor.
72 pages cm.
ISBN: 978-1-68019-863-3 paperback
       978-1-68019-869-0 ebook
       978-1-68019-870-6 ebook
1. Christianity. 2. Truth. 3. Supernatural.
I. Title
2017910063

TABLE OF CONTENTS

FOREWORD

Garry Sheaffer commissions his heart for the generations as he shares the importance of being filled with the Holy Spirit and developing the mindset of an overcomer. In his book, Above & Beyond, he shares his hope for the body of Christ to no longer stay stagnant in the things of the past but be fully unified. Through stories pulled from his own life experiences and backed with truth from scriptures, this book will show you how to go above your understanding, and beyond your expectations. You will gain new insight at the opportunity to experience Jesus for who He really is at the magnitude in which His heart not only longs to know you, but longs to be known by you.

–Team eGen

INTRODUCTION

Without continual pursuit, life can become dull, and the individual can become complacent, uninfluential, and ineffective in their God-given mission. Discontentment leads to a spirit of depression and heaviness, and many people abandon their spiritual walk with the Lord. They quit going to church and turn to other means of fulfillment and satisfaction, all of which fall short of their expectations, and, all too often, lead to a life of sin.

Most of us have gone through seasons where we question our call and purpose in life because of unexpected occurrences, those unplanned events that do not line up with what we had hoped for, thus leading to negative emotional responses. Moreover, there remains a hunger down deep inside our souls that keeps saying, "There's got to be something more, for God didn't bring me to this place in my life to tell me this is as good as it's going to get."

It takes perseverance, and endurance, and a willingness to discard all the ordinary and standard things that many settle for, and instead, pursue God's best for our lives. This doesn't come easy or without a cost. It may mean sacrifice of relationships and even a change of career and geographical location. God never said it was going to be without those types of challenges, but He did promise to go before us and also to be with us as Jehovah Jireh, our Provider.

All too often we think that because we're a born-again child of God, it's up to Him to just make it happen, to give us His very best, without any sacrifice on our part. But that's not going to happen. If something doesn't require a personal cost from us, we tend to devalue those things and take less responsibility to care for them. Anything that God has given to us has already come at a cost to Him, and we should respect those blessings and opportunities as being holy and precious.

During the years of my own personal walk with the Lord, I have lived through seasons of transition which have caused me to question God as to why something was happening. Those times also created a rash of different emotions, some good and some not so good.

But what I've found is that after all the uncertainty cleared, the path ahead opened up and actually initiated a promotion from the past season I had been in. God has promised that, if we are faithful in the small things, He will bless us with greater things.

I have found that there is a place with the Lord, as we walk with Him, that is *above our understanding and beyond our expectations.* God is looking for those who are willing to step out and trust Him with all that they are, then journey into unchartered territory to find the treasures of knowing Him more intimately, and finally tap into the unclaimed resources He has available for each of us. Will you be one of those who will continue to reach into the *above and beyond* of God?

I hope you enjoy your time reading some of the personal experiences I share in this book, so that perhaps you can avoid some of the mistakes I've made on my journey in order to fulfill God's purpose and destiny for my own life. If we could get a glimpse down the road a year from now, we might be amazed at what God has planned for you and me. Yet we might miss an opportunity if we choose to settle for less than His best!

CHAPTER 1
SEEKERS

I don't know about you, but I have this thing in me that likes to hunt for and uncover hidden treasures—to find things that may have been lost or abandoned. I enjoy watching shows where divers plunge into the ocean among vessels, which had been carrying gold and other treasures centuries ago, and recover these invaluable, ancient artifacts. In much the same way, that's what we are doing as we seek the Lord and the treasures of His Kingdom.

Matthew 6:33 says, "Seek ye first the kingdom of God, and His righteousness; and all these things shall be added unto you" (KJV). To "seek" means to search with the purpose of obtaining. It's putting forth an extra effort to get something that has seemed to be out of reach or hidden from our sight and ability to obtain. I don't know about you, but I want all that God has purposed for me!

For the past 20 years, I've been on a mission to come into the place of fullness in my journey with the Lord. It's not that I didn't love the Lord and serve Him prior to that time, but rather, other things, like my secular job and extracurricular activities, took much of my time and effort. Another issue that arose was the fact that, when I did come to a high point in my walk with the Lord, I found that it was actually only another plateau, with another mountain looming before me—which I had to likewise climb to get to another level.

Think of what life would be like if where you are right now is the final goal or destination, with nothing more to pursue or strive for. We would quickly become bored, discontented, and more than likely, complacent. I have been associated with people in ministry who were involved only for the salary or "did church" by following a book published by a denomination, which really didn't cause them to seek the Lord for themselves. It was a life of routine, tradition, and ritual, without the manifest presence of God. However, our God is a living God, and His Word, the Bible, is just as alive and powerful and active as He is. I don't mean to be critical or judgmental, but I believe God meant church and our time together to be energized by His very power and presence.

To live in the *above and beyond* of God requires a continual indulgence in His Word, in prayer with Him, in worship unto Him, and then believing that there are greater levels of impartation available than what we've already experienced. The anointing of the Lord is precious and costly. So if you genuinely want to possess that anointing, it will require a personal sacrifice of your commitment, time, effort, and resources. The question is, what value do you place in what God has given you and what He has made available to you?

In December of 2014, as I was being informed of my release from my pastoral duties at our church, a wonderful church by the way, I began to feel that God had something more, a new level of ministry for my wife and me. As ministers, we have to be careful not to become too comfortable where we are positioned and where we consequently refuse to move on to the greater things He has waiting for us. When this circumstance was happening, I remembered a story of the eagle, that when its young are ready to be released out of the nest, the adult eagle will nudge them out into a freefall, forcing them to learn how to fly. I kind of felt that way, for we had been in that particular church for 35 years, 16 years of which was in a pastoral role.

Immediately, I began searching for the new identity of ministry that God was calling us to. I felt kind of like Abraham, during the time when God told Him to *first go*—just simply begin to move, before He would show him where he was to eventually reside. That's a very uncomfortable place, because in most cases, we like to know all the details ahead of time.

In my own experience, during a Sunday night prayer gathering, which we had led for many years, I made a statement about "above and beyond," as I was conveying a thought God had given to me. Afterward, the following week, I was on the phone with a couple who at the time was leading the worship for our prayer meetings, and out of my mouth came that same statement—"above and beyond." In response, they said they believed this was the name of the ministry to which God was calling us as a couple.

I began to pray in that direction and eventually received God's confirmation to move forward. Thus, *Above and Beyond Ministries* was birthed. I am convinced that God has far more prepared for us—that which He wants to release in our lives—than what we presently are aware of. He is simply waiting for us to come and seek Him for the fullness, for the fulfillment of that hunger, and for a greater understanding of who He is and what He has for us.

The Scriptures that God has given me to affirm Above and Beyond Ministries speak volumes about God's desire to flood our lives with His presence, about that which will lead us into new territories and dimensions, and that which will carry us *above and beyond our present understanding and our expectations.* Considering our Bible colleges and seminaries, along with the advanced theological training and knowledge we can receive from them, we realize that they barely touch the surface of the depths of God's power, presence, and provision that He desires to bestow upon those who seek Him faithfully.

There is a world of lost souls out there and a multitude of wandering saints who are searching for that "something more" as I was. It's going to take people like you and me, who have pursued and who have found it, to assist them in likewise finding this spiritual treasure and "mining it up"! I pray you are one of those who God has been calling up. Perhaps you have been discontented with your position or your circumstances; maybe you're tired of the status quo and being politically correct. But now you're on a mission to lay claim to your portion of the treasures of His Kingdom that He has allotted to you!

I want to thank two personal friends, William and Deborah Fisher, who have been there to encourage and literally push my wife, Wanda, and me on in this journey to fulfillment; for they are continually urging us on this pathway, to seek and find the treasure of God's divine destiny for our lives. I pray that each of you who are reading this book have the blessing of friends, or will soon find companions like mine, who will not allow you to settle for less than God's best for you.

In Matthew chapter 7, we read Jesus' Sermon on the Mount, where He admonished those present regarding several areas of a lifestyle of prayer. He knew this knowledge was vital if they were to faithfully follow Him and likewise receive all He had for them. Specifically, He said in verses 7-8:

Ask, and it shall be given you; seek, and ye shall find; knock, and it shall be opened unto you: For every one that asketh receiveth; and he that seeketh findeth; and to him that knocketh it shall be opened (KJV).

Here we see three different levels of praying even as we reach out to our heavenly Father for His help. All too often people never move beyond just asking. If they don't receive almost instantly what they're desiring, they quickly give up and move on to other resources to fulfill their longing, yet are seldom satisfied or feel complete. But in verse 8, Jesus said that those who persisted, and continued to seek and knock, would find what they were looking for. I used to have an issue with losing, or should I say, misplacing my car keys and my wallet, and I would stop at nothing, regardless of how long it took, until I found them. What might God be able to do in our lives if we would, with that same intensity, seek Him and His destiny for our present and future endeavors!

So many people end up being underachievers and never fulfill God's will for their lives. These are good people with good intentions who truly know the Lord; unfortunately, they just fail to press in, to seek Him with all their hearts, and then find that place in Him that is *above their understanding and beyond their expectations.* If God says I can have it, then I definitely want it; and if God says I can do it, then let's get it done!

Yet there's so much hanging in the balance that depends upon our participation with regard to being "all in" and fulfilling His will. If you and I will answer His call, He will equip us to accomplish the task at hand. There are lost souls who need to hear the message of salvation, and there are sick people who need God's healing power. There are those bound by demonic strongholds and addictions who need to be set free. We are His servants, His hands extended, and His voice proclaiming the Good News to those who are in need. And we do so by delivering the truth, so that that truth can set them free. He's the power behind His Word. It's time to quit worrying about the outcome and leave the results up to Him, for He is faithful to do all He has promised.

The problem with most people, and I was guilty of this too, is that we're afraid God might not do what we're proclaiming; and then if He doesn't, we'll look bad. That's being fearful, proud, and self-centered. All of us have attempted things in life and have failed at some point, but when we operate in His power and authority, according to His will, He will never fail.

Great men and women who we read about in the Bible, who experienced and walked in the supernatural power of God, were those who first spent time seeking God, who heard from Him as to what direction to pursue and what plans to follow, and then stepped out in faith and did what He said to do. It means paying the price of sacrifice and dedication to His call. Jeremiah 29:13 says, "And ye shall seek Me, and find Me, when ye shall search for Me with all your heart" (KJV).

Ask yourself these questions: How much time do I spend worshipping Him, praying, and seeking His presence? Or is my prayer life built around words like "Give me this," "Lord, do that," "Help me with this"? I know this sounds a little harsh, but there comes a time when we need to take personal inventory as to where we are with regard to our spiritual growth and realize the adjustments we need to make on our end so that we may see His Kingdom come and His will be done in us and then through us. The Lord told us to love and seek Him with all our hearts. Hence, let your heart be filled to overflowing with His presence and power so that you then have the resources from which to make a withdrawal when needed.

Join with me and others who are feeling the urgency in our spirits and realize the lateness of the hour. Press into His presence like never before. As you do, God will open up the reservoir of His storehouse and pour out the fresh oil and the fresh fire of His Holy Spirit that will equip you for the journey ahead—a journey of supernatural proportion that will take you *above and beyond*! So come on, and let's get started!

I want to end this chapter with one of my favorite verses found in the Gospel of Matthew—the words of Jesus Himself:

But seek ye first the Kingdom of God, and His righteousness; and all these things shall be added unto you (Matthew 6:33 KJV).

CHAPTER 2

ACTIVATING GOD'S WORD INTO OUR JOURNEY

As you begin this new journey of pursuit into the *above and beyond* of God, let's look at the foundational Scriptures that have inspired my own journey, helping me stay focused on God's plan and destiny. I believe that whatever we do, it should be based on and built around the Word of God, for His Word will never fail us or return to Him void.

One of the initial verses He gave me is Ephesians 3:20:

> *Now to Him who is able to do exceedingly abundantly above all that we ask or think, according to the power that works in us* (NKJV).

In this chapter of Ephesians, the Apostle Paul is encouraging the believers at Ephesus and speaks to them about the mysteries of Christ and how the Lord has made those things known to him through revelation knowledge.

Beginning in verse 14, he turns the encouragement into a prayer for them and then asks the Lord to strengthen their inner man in verse 16. Subsequently, he expounds on God's ability to do "exceedingly abundantly above" all that they can ask or think, according to the power that is at work in them. I don't know about you, but I can ask for some pretty big things, and when it comes to thinking big thoughts, wow, I can really get carried away. But, here, Paul is telling them that the God they are serving can go way beyond any of their requests.

We cannot measure God's abilities in earthly terms. No matter how hard we try, God will exceed those numbers in height, depth, width, and length. God goes to the nth degree to care for and meet the needs of His children; yet He still desires of us to ask in faith, and then, upon receiving, give Him thanks for responding. Have you ever stopped to wonder where you might be today if it weren't for the Lord in your life? That's a scary thought. He has been so good to us and will continue to be faithful.

Another verse He has given me that expresses His provision for the road ahead is found in First Corinthians 2:9:

> *But as it is written, Eye hath not seen, nor ear heard, neither have entered into the heart of man, the things which God hath prepared for them that love Him* (KJV).

Here, Paul is addressing a church, the church at Corinth, and speaking about the wisdom of God. Once again he is referring to it as a mystery. Merriam-Webster defines *mystery* as "a religious truth known by revelation alone, something not understood or beyond understanding."

We, in our generation, have seen such great advancement in technology—computers, i-pads, smart phones—the list goes on and on. Anytime we want to know or learn about something, we can pick up our laptop or smart phone, punch in the question, and within seconds, out comes the answer. We likewise have many tools that we can use to interpret Scripture and unveil the meaning of the Word of God. These include different versions of the Bible and commentaries, along with the internet. Still, there are truths that God has withheld for such a time as this, and He is revealing them even in this hour through you and me to confirm His Word and advance His Kingdom in the earth.

God has placed at our disposal even more treasures, which we need to mine in this hour, to assist us in reaching and transforming lives. We have been given access to these treasures so that we may help others find that "something more" they are searching for. Yet all too often we keep asking God to do what He has always done, in the same way He has done it, not expecting anything to change, but presuming the same-old, same-old. I hear people say, "Bring us back to old-time Pentecost as it was 50 or 60 years ago." But our God is not into repetition. I love what He says in Jeremiah 33:3: "Call unto Me, and I will answer thee, and shew thee great and mighty things, which thou knowest not." (KJV) that's not repetition!

Likewise, in First Corinthians 2:9, God tells us that there are things that no human eye has seen, no human ear has heard, and no human heart (mind) has thought. These are things that God has previously prepared, which He would now like to reveal to a candidate who truly loves Him, and through whom He can release. I personally believe, and have stated it on many occasions, that our greatest days are yet ahead as we approach the end of this age and the return of our Lord and Savior Jesus Christ. My only concern is this—why would we want anything less than God's best? I don't want to be just an observer, but rather a participator in all that God is doing and going to do, in things that are *above our understanding and beyond our expectations*!

Even as we see the wisdom and creativity of man increase in our own generation, through so many channels, still it will not compare with what God is going to unveil to His true Church in this hour. Take time to pray and ask the Lord to use you so that you might be the conduit that He and His miraculous supernatural power flow through, that you may see signs, wonders, and miracles released wherever He sends you.

He is coming back for a glorious Church, a victorious Church, without spot or wrinkle, not a broken-down, defeated Church. You would have to agree with me that the Church in its present state is not there yet. Nonetheless, God is calling His apostles and prophets to go forth and speak words of life that will bring transformation to the Body of Christ so that she can reach the multitude of lost souls and hasten the Lord's coming. He will come for a Bride whose lamps are ready and trimmed, full of oil and burning brightly, who is watching, waiting, and ready for His return.

The Word of God is so crucial to the life and health of the believer. Everything we say and do must align with His Word. Accordingly, soul prosperity should come before material wealth. Third John 1:2 says, "Beloved, I wish above all things that thou mayest prosper and be in health, even as thy soul prospereth" (KJV). Yet you cannot prosper, nor can God's Word accomplish anything if it remains on the coffee table or our bookshelves. Rather, it must be read and then activated for it to bear fruit and to be fulfilled before our eyes. Furthermore, it is to be the very weapon that will withstand any assault or accusation of the enemy.

In addition, Hebrews 4:12 says, "For the word of God is quick, and powerful, and sharper than any twoedged sword, piercing even to the dividing asunder of soul and spirit, and of the joints and marrow, and is a discerner of the thoughts and intents of the heart" (KJV). That pretty much covers the whole of life as we know it. There's not one area where the Word of God cannot affect our lives, even down to our thought life. I often encourage people as they pray, to pray the Word of God over their lives and circumstances. You cannot pray amiss if you pray God's Word back to Him. Find verses of Scripture that pertain to the issues you are facing and then apply God's Word as the antidote. It will bring healing, wholeness, and restoration.

John penned these words in John chapter 1: "In the beginning was the Word, and the Word was with God, and the Word was God" (John 1:1 KJV). Then in verse 14 he said, "And the Word was made flesh, and dwelt among us...." You see, He's not only the God of the Word, but He *is* the Word. That's what makes it so powerful. His very integrity and character hang on His Word! God's Word is eternal and will remain after everything else is over and done. In Matthew 24:35, Jesus said, "Heaven and earth shall pass away, but My words shall not pass away" (KJV). God created the heavens and the earth by just speaking a word, and down through the ages of time, His Word continues to be fulfilled. Much of the Bible was written prophetically of things that have not yet occurred but are for another time. Even now, God has appointed modern-day prophets who hear from the Lord and then speak what He tells them. These words of prophecy are powerful, giving hope and direction to the Church and to the child of God. Many of the transitions that I have personally gone through have been bathed with prophetic words from trustworthy men and women of God. It is also important to remember that prophetic words will never contradict the written Word of God, but always confirm it.

I want to encourage you to study the Word of God wholeheartedly, know what it says, know how it applies to your own life, as well as how to apply it—and God will bring it to pass. But be careful, for there are those who want to take small portions of it and make it say what they want it to say in order to use it for their own gain. But it will never profit them anything, for God knows the thoughts and intents of the heart and will not allow His Word to be misused. God states in Revelation 22:19 that He will take away anyone's part in His holy city if they take anything away from His Word.

Activation is a powerful weapon. Jesus used it to defeat satan when satan tried to tempt Him in the wilderness. Likewise, His Word is sufficient for you and me. Therefore, it's up to you and me to do our part, to study it, to know it, and to activate it—to be doers of the Word and not hearers only. Know that God will do exceedingly abundantly above what we ask or think, and that we have not yet beheld, whether it be through seeing, hearing, or comprehending, all that God has prepared for those who love Him. I believe God is about to release a new level and a greater anointing upon His Bride, His Church!

CHAPTER 3

WE'RE OPERATING ON GOD'S TIME CLOCK

Along the pathway, we all have faced some disappointing events or occurrences, things that seemed to have detoured us from our destination. But many times, God has used and continues to use these "disappointments" as divine appointments. What seems like a setback, often becomes a setup by God to bring us into the fullness of His call upon our lives.

We used to sing an old chorus in a youth group back in the 60's that said, "The Lord knows the way through the wilderness, all we have to do is follow." When our best-laid plans lead us into territory that seems like a maze with only dead ends, it's here where we need to look to the Lord and trust Him to show us the path to take that will bring us to our destination and ensure that we arrive right on time.

When the ways of man and the decisions others make seem to derail and detour our pathway, God can immediately begin to recalibrate our course and bring us back into alignment with His will for us. How often have decisions, which were made outside of our ability to change, altered our life and journey? The next time a circumstance like this occurs, we need to approach it with the right attitude, knowing that God is there working matters in our favor, and meanwhile, be patient and submissive as He blazes a new trail for us to take.

I love the verses in Jeremiah 29:11-13, which say:

For I know the thoughts that I think toward you, saith the Lord, thoughts of peace, and not of evil, to give you an expected end. Then shall ye call upon Me, and ye shall go and pray unto Me, and I will hearken unto you. And ye shall seek Me, and find Me, when ye shall search for Me with all your heart (KJV).

Really, the only one who can stop you from achieving and reaching the finish line is you, yourself, when you give up or allow these inconveniences to cause you to quit. God's plans always remain active and available, but He also needs your cooperation!

In the three verses of Jeremiah printed above, God gives us the directives we need to navigate through those disruptions. He encourages us to seek Him with all our heart, pursue His presence, and then watch how He works on our behalf to take what may have seemed to be impossible circumstances and bring about events or opportunities that are above and beyond anything we could have imagined.

Just a few chapters later, in Jeremiah 33, we find another favorite verse of mine. Here God gives us another promise of revealing those things of which we have no previous knowledge.

Call unto Me, and I will answer thee, and show thee great and mighty things, which thou knowest not (Jeremiah 33:3 KJV).

You see, friend, God is always one step ahead of us, preparing a way and a place for us to enter into a new realm of His power and glory, and to participate in the mysteries that He is presently unveiling, which are likewise important to the whole of what He's doing. And this is the neat part—He wants you and me to have a role. God is positioned and ready to answer our prayers, but we must request His assistance, as well as learn to put aside our willfulness and determination to do it our own way. We must choose to walk in obedience to Him, in His timing and manner in which He decides to take us. This is never an easy course to take, especially if our lives have been filled with failed relationships and ventures due to decisions other people have made, which have adversely affected our lives. Our trust is earned by others; so when it is violated, a wall of mistrust takes its place. However, God wants to tear down that wall in order to give you access into His destiny, which has been reserved just for you, for such a time as this.

We must realize that the God who said He would reveal great and might things (which we're not presently aware of) is the same God of all creation speaking. We have no idea how massive those things are nor of the impact that they will have in the days ahead—things which will not only affect us but also those whom God wants us to minister to. His abilities to produce what He promises goes way beyond our ability to even imagine or think. Wow! *Above our understanding and beyond our expectations!*

If you are ready to take your journey into the *above and beyond*—that place which God wants to reveal to you and to prepare you for, I want to give you some simple steps to help you get started. First of all, do a personal evaluation of your present situation, your relationship with the Lord, your circumstances that lay before you, and how you got to this point. Also assess what your plans are to move forward.

All too often we fall into the trap of routine, trying to do it the way we've always done it, the same-old, same-old clichés, yet expect different results than the last time. To get something you've never had, you have to do something you've never done before, and in ways that may seem strange and challenging to you.

I believe all of us, if we're honest with ourselves and the Lord, are ready for a personal transformation to take place, a renewing of our minds that will bring about a shift in how we think and do things. But we have to want something bad enough in order to pursue it with unrelenting desire, and then holding nothing back. They often say in the gym, "No pain, no gain!"

Take a good look at where you are and then go to step two: Begin to pray relentlessly and ask God what He'd have you do as you prepare to move forward. Begin to cooperate with the direction the Holy Spirit leads you in. Remember that your journey is a marathon and not a sprint, which means that not only do you need to know the method of how to move, but also the timing of each step you take. Some days, it may involve standing still, some in walking, and at other times God may ask you to run. Stay in sync with the Lord. Good things, or should I say, great things usually don't happen overnight, so learn to wait, listen, and then make your move.

A good Scripture to refer to at this time is Isaiah 40:31: "But they that wait upon the Lord shall renew their strength; they shall mount up with wings as eagles; they shall run, and not be weary; and they shall walk, and not faint" (KJV). Great things come to those who wait.

Step three involves that very same thought, some of which was involved in step two—*anticipation*. Another word for *anticipation* is *faith*. Live each day with the expectation that this could be the day that God delivers on all that He has presently promised. So often, God is a slow cooker and not a microwaver. If what God has promised you is worth having, it is also worth waiting for. Many years ago, there was a statement often repeated: "If God said it, I believe it, and that settles it!" May that be how we approach this new season in our lives. Unfortunately, though, so many people become impatient on their journey and give up on the brink of their miracle, just before their breakthrough moment. Don't be one of them.

Capture a mental picture of what God has spoken to you or has begun to reveal to you, and then daily pray and remind yourself that it is going to happen. In the meantime, remind yourself that it's worth waiting for. Don't let anyone talk you out of it or tell you that you could never be this or never do that. God is not a God that He would lie to you. Remember, a spacious building has never been erected overnight. Rather, the owner of the property begins with a vision of what he wants to build, then hires an architect to design and draw the structure on a blueprint. Afterward, the different stages of the building process are laid out so that those who are eventually hired are aware of their specific duties. Then the construction begins.

The land is cleared, and the footers are dug and poured. The foundation wall that will support the building is laid. Then the actual structure is erected, including the walls, the exterior, and the interior; and the building begins to take shape. Then it's time to put on the finishing touches, which will involve many more decisions in order to create the beauty and effect that the owner is looking for. Finally, the rooms with be furnished with the appropriate items, bringing forth the product that the owner desired from the beginning.

Each step will take many weeks, some many months, depending on the magnitude of the building, or the dream, before it becomes a reality.

And now we come to step four—*activation*, or the grand opening. You must stay fully involved in this process and continue to pray every day, speaking forth what God has promised, regardless of any setbacks or delays. Because I worked in the building trade for many years, I know there will be times such as these to deal with. Ultimately, though, the building will be completed.

Be a Nehemiah and stay focused. Stay on the wall of your dream. Be committed to your call, and be prepared to face the opposition that may arise in the process. There may be those, even good people, who won't want you to succeed, many who have abandoned their own dreams and won't want you to accomplish what they couldn't seem to achieve.

Nevertheless, God will use these times of change and transition to build faith, strength, and endurance in you for the new season ahead, which will be useful when the next big transition comes. Everything God does is progressive, from glory to glory, and strength to strength. If, however, God would show us the whole scenario of our life from start to finish, that which He has planned out, we'd never believe it would be possible. That's why He gives us one layer at a time.

Then, there will come that day, when we cross the true finish line, when we get the call to "Come up hither, there are some things I'd like to show you." Remember the words of the Apostle Paul in Philippians 3:12-14:

> *Not as though I had already attained, either were already perfect: but I follow after, if that I may apprehend that for which also I am apprehended of Christ Jesus. Brethren, I count not myself to have apprehended: but this one thing I do, forgetting those things which are behind, and reaching forth unto those things which are before, I press toward the mark for the prize of the high calling of God in Christ Jesus* (KJV).

Finally, step five—arriving at our destination, the place of *completion*. This will be the day when you can look back over the entire journey and see how the hand of the Lord led you and provided for you every step of the way. God does not make mistakes. He remembers the gifting and ability He gave you when He formed you in your mother's womb. And He will be there to bring you into maturity, on His time clock, into the fullness of His call upon your life. It will be a day, an endless day of celebration, when you'll be able to say, "It has been worth it all!"

CHAPTER 4

ENGAGING THE SUPERNATURAL

The generation with whom we are living is seeking to experience supernatural power. Sadly, though, they are looking for it in all the wrong places, and satan is more than accommodating, providing power through works of evil, such as witchcraft, satanism, and the occult. People pay significant amounts of money to learn of their future and to possess this supernatural power. However, what satan does is counterfeit and distorts what God intended to be used for good. Even so, many are deceived.

It's time for the Church of Jesus Christ to awaken from its spiritual slumber, to realize the call of God upon the Body, and begin to operate in His supernatural authority and power in the earth. Christ has authorized us and given us the "keys of the Kingdom of God" to bind the powers of darkness, to loose the power of God through the work of the Holy Spirit, and to finish the call of God He has placed on the Church. It's called the Great Commission!

A large percentage of churches, though, have succumbed to the pressures of certain minority groups which have abandoned the principles of God's Word, the Bible, and instead promote their own agendas. In doing so, they have established no spiritual authority, influence, or credibility in their communities. Therefore, my mission is to reignite a fresh fire and passion for the presence of God and to release the power of the Holy Spirit into the Body of Christ.

The Church needs to repent for their failure to do God's will and ask the Lord to breathe His breath of life back into them—with that same resurrection power that raised Jesus from the dead, as spoken about in Ezekiel chapter 37. When Ezekiel prophesied to the winds, God breathed new life into them, and they became a "great and mighty army." I believe this is a picture of the last-day Church whom God desires to raise up. We likewise must remind ourselves of the Scripture of First John 4:4b: "Greater is He that is in you, than he that is in the world" (KJV).

There is a remnant Bride of Christ arising at this hour, and we need to ask ourselves the question: "Will I be one of them?" These will be a people who will carry the breaker anointing, who will invade the enemy strongholds—cities and regions that have been in control of evil influences for many generations; and they will take back what the enemy has stolen from those generations. They will be a supernatural force that lives outside the boundaries and limitations that ungodly governments and systems would try to place on them. They will be a people who not only know about the power of God, but will operate in an *above-and-beyond* realm of understanding and expectation of those who are refusing to arise.

You may ask me, "What's it going to take for me to be one of those individuals chosen to carry this last-day anointing?" I'm so glad you asked! It's going to take an all-out, nothing-held-back commitment and dedication of our lives to the Lord Jesus Christ. It's going to take a sacrifice of our time, spending it in prayer, seeking the Lord, hearing His voice, receiving His strategies necessary for the journey ahead, and then having Him equip and empower us with a spirit of wisdom, boldness, and supernatural strength to fulfill His purposes and plans. That's all!

Focus

Focus will be a key as we move forward. I think of David and his mighty men who returned from battle to find their homes destroyed. Families had been taken hostage and their possessions stolen by the Amalekites. They were devastated and angry. David's own men had thoughts of killing him. "But..." we read in First Samuel, "David encouraged himself in the Lord his God" (1 Samuel 30:6b KJV). David asked the priest for the ephod, a priestly apron or breastplate that only the high priest wore. Verse 8 then says: "And David enquired at the Lord, saying, Shall I pursue after this troop? Shall I overtake them? And He answered him; Pursue: for thou shalt surely overtake them, and without fail recover all" (1 Samuel 30:8 KJV).

Here we find an example to follow when confronted with difficult circumstances. Many have had great plans for the future and have worked hard to get there only to have their hopes and dreams stolen or dashed by the enemy. When he, the devil, becomes aware of the plans God has for us, he will try to hijack them and steal them from us. All too often, when this happens, many give up hope and just shut down and quit.

We must be aware and cautious, that as a child of God, we have an enemy whose desire it is "...to steal, and to kill, and to destroy" (John 10:10a KJV); and realize that he will stop at nothing to accomplish this destruction. Bad things happen to good people all the time. It's part of this journey of life. Satan knows that if you find and fulfill God's purposes and destiny, your life will do great damage to the kingdom of darkness. That is why he works so hard to stop you. But when we get our focus off the circumstances and onto the Lord, He promises, "I am come that they might have life, and that they might have it more abundantly" (John 10:10b KJV).

If, however, we continue to allow the devil to rob us of our God-given destiny and the resources to accomplish it, he will be all too happy to accommodate us. He longs to destroy your relationship with the Lord. Moreover, he will try to convince you it is God who is causing these bad things to happen to you. The fact is, though, it is the devil who will try to rob you of your health through worry, fear, anger, and depression, as well as rob you of your means to succeed and be an overcomer.

First John 3:8 says:

He that committeth sin is of the devil; for the devil sinneth from the beginning. For this purpose the Son of God was manifested, that he might destroy the works of the devil.

Friend, God stands ready to aid you, not only by recovering your losses and restoring them back into your hands, but He also desires to reveal hidden treasures from prior generations that lay unclaimed in your family lineage.

Commitment

All too often Christians develop the mindset that because they are saved, God has a responsibility to provide everything they need, and sometimes want, without any further surrender and commitment on their part. This is only a partial truth. God does indeed want to meet and supply all our needs, and often does so in spite of our lukewarm lifestyle. Still, we, as born-again Christians, need to grow up and come to a place of maturity in our daily relationship with Him.

Commitment is a word many people either don't understand, or because of the fear of what it might cost them, avoid it all together. I see so many people whose only spiritual goal is to be saved and go to Heaven, which is all well and good in that sense, but they miss out on much of the greater expectations of God. This type of selfish lifestyle leads only to more frustration and disappointment, and causes people to actually question God's faithfulness. However, the problem is not on God's side of the relationship. I have often told people that God is never early or late, but right on time every time, according to His discretion in each situation. The issue is our own decision to *not* give of ourselves.

Commitment, according to Webster's Dictionary, means "to put in charge of or trust, to transfer or consign, to pledge." When we commit our lives to the Lord, we turn over what was solely ours to Him and then choose to walk in obedience and faithfulness to His leadership. God is not a spiritual Santa Claus who is obligated to fulfill all our wants and wishes and desires. If you want to receive all of Him and all that He has for you, then you need to give Him *all of you*!

Psalm 37:5 says, "Commit thy way unto the Lord; trust also in Him; and He shall bring it to pass" (KJV). Committing means "letting go of or giving up control of," and then allowing the Lord to navigate the course ahead for you. He's not your co-pilot; He's your pilot! Proverbs 3:6 says, "In all thy ways acknowledge Him, and He shall direct thy paths" (KJV).

One of the hardest choices for me to make is to give up control; for example, to get out from behind the wheel, and to let someone else drive the car when we travel. It is very seldom that I let Wanda, my wife, drive when we go on trips. No one knows how to drive the way that I like to drive, and that person just might make a wrong turn, miss the exit, and get us lost (as if I have never done the same). Believe me, friends, God will never miss the exit or take you down the wrong road; for He's already been there preparing the way, and

He knows what lies ahead. Follow Him as He leads you in His paths of righteousness.

We miss out on so much of the joy in the journey when we are constantly bothered about the details. We miss a lot of the "scenery" along the way as well as the opportunities to touch others and experience the release of God's supernatural power in us and through us. Doing it "my way" is not always the best way.

For years, I worked in the construction trade, building churches, commercial properties, and then residential homes. At that time, I was extremely committed to my job, always working hard, and would go the extra mile to please my company and our customers. I was taught a great work ethic over the years by those who employed me and those who worked with me, and now, I can apply those traits to ministry.

But there is also a caution with regard to hard work: We must not become so committed to the mission that we neglect spending time with the One who has called us and who sends us forth. God should have first place in all we do. If, however, we become so busy working, we set ourselves up for failure and disappointment. He is not a hard taskmaster, so we likewise don't have to stress ourselves out trying to please Him. Moreover, it is not so important that we operate in His supernatural power, for He can shut us down very quickly. Rather, He simply craves our personal attention and spending time with us.

Perseverance

Also important in walking in the supernatural power of God is learning to *persevere* during the tough, dry times until the breakthrough comes. Timing, once again, is crucial on this journey to fulfilling God's will and purposes. Think about Joseph for a moment. God gave him several dreams about his future and destiny, but remember what he had to go through to get there. He suffered the hatred of his brothers, was thrown into a pit, sold into slavery in a foreign land, was falsely accused and tossed into prison, and consequently almost forgotten. All this happened over a span of several years before he finally arrived at his ultimate destiny, one in which he once again had to face his brothers. But God was faithful all along the way and continuously used Joseph in all types of situations to touch the people around him. He was a born leader who learned to persevere.

Remember, the greater the call of God is on your life, the greater the resistance will be from the enemy and his determination to try to hinder or stop you—even from those who are close to you. When we enlisted in this journey with the Lord, He didn't say it was going to be easy or that everything would fall right into place without any opposition. So to endure through the trials, you need to develop a perseverance—a faith in God, a maturity for the fulfillment of the call, and a greater measure of strength to overcome every setback along the way.

Perseverance means to persist in spite of the obstacles we encounter along the way. I could tell you story after story of things that have happened in my own life on the journey to where the Lord has led me today. My experiences may not have been as severe as Joseph's, but they still created a lot of wonderment on my part as to how all of this could work for my good. There were those times when I felt like giving up and quitting, dropping out of the race, especially when opposition arose from those I least expected it. Many times it even came from within the church, which made it even more difficult to handle. At all times, we have to remember that we're vulnerable, and at a weak moment, by letting our guard down, can fall prey to the tactics of the enemy. Rather than hold bitterness or seek vengeance, I've learned to forgive those who have mistreated me, or who misunderstood my heart, or those who spoke against me and falsely accused me.

In Joseph's life, several years down the road, he was given an opportunity to get even with his brothers, but rather than seek revenge, he chose to forgive them and allowed the Lord to use him to not only spare their lives but those of a whole nation during a severe famine. We likewise might never know the magnitude of what God has in store for us when He calls us; but if we persevere and press through those seemingly impossible situations, God will bring us to that same place He brought Joseph, and many lives will be touched in the process.

God has told us in His Word that there will definitely be perilous times, times of adversity along the way. None of us are exempt.

Which means that we must treasure even more our personal relationship with Him and continue to draw closer and closer to Him. Frustrations and hardships will come and go, but His presence will never leave us. He will never forsake us. Let those disappointments become God's divine appointments along the way.

Hold on, my friend, for joy comes in the morning. The darkest hour is just before dawn breaks, and a new day will unfold before you. If you are in such a place, frustrated and overwhelmed by your present circumstances, most likely your moment of breakthrough is knocking on the door; and your destiny, which was once a prophetic word or a dream from the Lord, is about to become reality. Persevere and press on, for the palace awaits your arrival!

CHAPTER 5

DEVELOPING AN OVERCOMER'S LIFESTYLE

One of my favorite chapters in the Bible is Romans 8. This entire chapter contains so many of God's promises to us as we face some of life's fiercest battles. Needless to say, we should become aware of what the Lord has made available to us in these difficult times, so that we avoid becoming a victim and casualty of the schemes and devices of the enemy.

Satan is the accuser of the brethren, but in Romans 8:1, Paul says,

There is therefore now no condemnation to them which are in Christ Jesus, who walk not after the flesh, but after the Spirit (KJV).

It is imperative that we get our minds cleared as to where we stand in our relationship with the Lord. First and foremost, we need to know our spiritual identity. To be able to move to the next level in our relationship with the Lord, we need to rid ourselves of any question with regard to who we are in Christ Jesus. This is the same area where satan attacked Eve in the Garden of Eden and questioned the authority of God's word to Adam and Eve—specifically the time when God told them that the one tree was off limits to them.

One of the major problems in the church as a whole today is a lack of true identity, in not knowing who we are in Christ, and being unfamiliar with the authority and power that come with that identity. Satan has convinced many that God doesn't really care about them, because if God did really care, they wouldn't be dealing with the problems they have. At other times, satan will tell people that they've gone too far away from God, and consequently, God has abandoned them without the hope of restoration. In fact, satan will even try to convince them that God is against them rather than for them.

Here's where knowing the Scripture is vital in overcoming these accusations. Jesus is our best example—He defeated the devil's on-slaught during His own temptation in the Wilderness by quoting the Word of God. He refused to succumb when satan tempted Him to stray from His destiny and pledge allegiance to him (see Matthew 4). Also take time to read Romans 8:31-39, for here Paul addresses just about any issue that could arise to hinder us from moving into the fullness of God's destiny and blessings for our lives.

Let me say this, as long as we are alive in these physical bodies on this earth, we will face opposition. You can't avoid it, but you can surely overcome it. Some of the greatest advancements in my life have come in the midst of some of the fiercest battles. You can't have a victory without a battle, and you can't have a testimony without a test! Satan will pull out every trick in his book to keep you from what God is calling you to, and he will even use those individuals close to you to accomplish his goal if possible. Remember, Jesus' road to victory took Him by way of the cross. Think about where you and I would be today if He had failed to accomplish that part of the Father's will.

In John chapter 16, Jesus also spoke about tribulations to His disciples:

These things I have spoken unto you, that in Me ye might have peace. In the world ye shall have tribulation: but be of good cheer; I have overcome the world (John 16:33 KJV).

Some of the most difficult days that this world has ever experienced are upon us right now; but if our lives are hidden in Christ and if He is truly the Lord of our lives, we will have a peace in the inner man that will sustain us in the midst of it all. Christ has already conquered death, hell, and the grave, and He has broken the power of the spirit of fear. Now, we have become the beneficiaries of His finished work of the cross.

Each of us has a choice to make. We can choose to allow present circumstances and the outside world to dictate how we feel, drive our emotions into a state of fear and hopelessness, and lead us to depression; or we can choose to commit our lives totally to the Lord and dwell in the secret place of His presence, abiding continually under the shadow of Almighty God. I like the latter option myself!

For too long we have been living and finding our identity in what others have said or by the events that occur in our lives, whether good or bad. But once again, we need to look into the Word of God and find out what He has already said we are. Consider Paul's words:

Nay, in all these things we are more than conquerors through Him that loved us (Romans 8:37 KJV).

Here, once again, we find another part of our identity. We are "more than conquerors." Likewise, Revelation 1:6 says, "[He] hath made us kings and priests unto God and His Father; to Him be glory and dominion for ever and ever. Amen" (KJV).

It's time to renounce the lies of the enemy and the false opinions of others, and begin to live in the truth of God's Word. It's time to be the head and not the tail, above and not beneath. God has higher expectations for us than we have for ourselves. Put the past and all of its pains and disappointments behind you and leave them buried there, no longer resurrecting them to relive the pain. Start dwelling in the awesome provision for which God has set you apart. It's time to venture *above and beyond* and into the realm of God's supernatural presence.

As I began this chapter, I mentioned Romans chapter 8 in which Paul wrote quite a bit about those who still based their lives on the laws of the Old Testament handed down through the generations. He also addressed how God sent His only Son (verse 3) to fulfill the law in us through Christ's righteousness, walking not after the flesh but after the Spirit.

In verse 6, Paul continued, "For to be carnally minded is death; but to be spiritually minded is life and peace"; and he mentioned that those who operated in the flesh would never please God (verse 8). Then, in verses 9-10, Paul wrote:

But ye are not in the flesh, but in the Spirit, if so be that the Spirit of God dwell in you. Now if any man have not the Spirit of Christ, he is none of His. And if Christ be in you, the body is dead because of sin; but the Spirit is life because of righteousness (KJV).

Thus, if we are going to be overcomers for Christ, we need to develop a new mindset, a renewed mind, and be rid of the fleshly ways of our past. We literally have to die to self-will and the flesh. It's in this transition that an identity shift occurs, for as we are now led by the Spirit of God, we are also the "sons of God" (verse 14). In verse 17, Paul went on to say: "And if children, then heirs; heirs of God, and joint-heirs with Christ; if so be that we suffer with Him, that we may be also glorified together." Do you realize the implications of being an heir of God and what that opens up to you? What is His, His Kingdom and power, is now ours also.

Jesus's purpose in coming was to save us, to raise us up with a new identity, and use us to advance His Kingdom in the earth. Do you realize, in the midst of all the chaos in the world today, that the creation itself is groaning for the revealing of the true sons of God?

Romans 8:19 and 22 states:

For the earnest expectation of the creature waiteth for the manifestation of the sons of God. ... For we know that the whole creation groaneth and travaileth in pain together until now (KJV).

A lot can change in a hurry if this revealing suddenly becomes reality.

In verse 26, Paul went on to speak about the involvement of the Holy Spirit through prayer:

Likewise the Spirit also helpeth our infirmities: for we know not what we should pray for as we ought: but the Spirit itself maketh intercession for us with groanings which cannot be uttered (KJV).

This is why it's important, and even vital, that we be filled with the Holy Spirit and learn to pray in our prayer language as we intercede for God's will to be done in the earth. All too often, most Christians never get past the "Now I lay me down to sleep" level of prayer, because they have not received the fullness of the Holy Spirit into their lives. Friend, that level of prayer, even though it is good, will not bring breakthrough, nor will it defeat the enemy who is coming against us and the Church.

But, if we will take time to press in to the presence of the Lord and allow the Holy Spirit to take the lead as we pray, then we will see the fulfillment of these Scriptures, especially the promise found in verse 28, one of the most quoted verses, where we read:

And we know that all things work together for good to them that love God, to them who are the called according to His purpose (KJV).

God has great plans for your life, a future and a hope, but it comes only through much prayer, and through trials and tribulations. Be assured, also, that with the assistance of the Holy Spirit, we will accomplish that purpose God has set before us.

I love these next few verses as Paul concludes this eighth chapter.

What shall we then say to these things? If God be for us, who can be against us? ... Who shall separate us from the love of Christ? shall tribulation, or distress, or persecution, or famine, or nakedness, or peril, or sword? ... Nay, in all these things we are more than conquerors through Him that loved us (Romans 8:31 and 37 KJV).

We have no legitimate excuse to fail or lose in the journey of life, for God has given us all we need to succeed and be an overcomer. You see, it is through the finished work of Christ, His death, resurrection, and ascension that we have been promised the victory. Because He overcame, we too can overcome whatever lies before us. There is nothing—nothing that should be able to derail you from fulfilling God's call upon your life.

And now let's look at the final two verses and see what our response should be, as it was for Paul.

For I am persuaded, that neither death, nor life, nor angels, nor principalities, nor powers, nor things present, nor things to come, nor height, nor depth, nor any other creature, shall be able to separate us from the love of God, which is in Christ Jesus our Lord (Romans 8:38 and 39 KJV).

It's time for us to rise up with a renewed determination to fulfill God's will and destiny for us and for those who God wants to touch through us. There are souls hanging in the balance who need to hear the Word of the Lord and the testimony of His saints, which will cause the harvest to be gathered. God's power is greater than that of the enemy. Accordingly, He has deputized each of us and given us His authority and power to carry out His will in the earth. The enemy's power is limited, compared to God's power; still, we must be careful not to take lightly his ability to deceive us. For his goal is "to steal, and to kill, and to destroy" (John 10:10 KJV) the saints of God and any other that would oppose his advances.

Let's believe we are who the Lord and His Word says we are. Let's believe we can do what His Word says we can do. Let's be all He says we can be and drive the enemy crazy trying to figure out a way to stop us. We are more than conquerors through Christ Jesus, and we overcome by the blood of the Lamb and the word of our testimony, and are willing, if necessary, to lay down our lives for the cause of the Gospel of Jesus Christ!

CHAPTER 6

SOMETHING MORE

The journey of life is like taking a cross-country trip, experiencing the landscape along the way and admiring the beauty of God's creation. As you travel, there will be hills and valleys, plains and plateaus, and even a desert place here and there, each one evoking a certain feeling, positive or negative. There will be those places and times that when we look back, we'll remember the beauty and splendor of God's created power. And then there will be those places or atmospheres that cause us to want to rush on by, to try to forget, because they will create a negative response, perhaps one of lifelessness or a feeling of depression and hopelessness. Even so, because we were set on a course to reach a destination, we continued to press forward and move through those areas on our journey.

This continues to be very much what our lives are like, from day to day, on our journey to fulfillment and eventually eternity. I can look back over the decades of my own life and list several scenarios or events that had positive, negative, or both positive and negative results, some of which I wish I could have avoided or detoured around. Yet I have found that, in the midst of them, God was constantly faithful to help me navigate through and toward better and greater things.

Many times we find ourselves in those places because of personal choices we have made, actions we wanted to take, rather than do what God was asking us to do. Then there were those times that the Lord led us to places that challenged us and caused us to take inventory of who we were and where we were headed. This is when we remember the words of David in Psalm 23:4: "Yea though I walk through the valley of the shadow of death, I will fear no evil: for Thou art with me; Thy rod and Thy staff they comfort me." God has purpose in all that He does and in the way that He leads. All we have to do is learn to follow.

There were many times that I chose to go my own way and do my own thing, while ignoring God's chosen pathway; and each time there were consequences to those choices. Sometimes I found myself in unfamiliar territory among unfriendly foes, some seen and others unseen. I call them destiny thieves whose main goal is to rob us of our purpose and destiny, which God has established for us, and thereby also taking away our peace and joy.

Much of life is experienced through trial and error until we finally learn to walk in obedience to the Holy Spirit's leading. Even then, we still have to navigate some rough terrain but will have a completely different attitude and mindset, which will lead to a totally different outcome. Life is truly a marathon and not a sprint! Every phase of the journey provides opportunities to mature as well as access the hidden treasures God has placed along the way that will make it all worth the journey.

Sometimes, troubles will come when we become comfortable in a certain place, or when we decide, *This is it, I've reached the pinnacle*. It's in this place where all kinds of attitudes and moods begin to attach themselves to us that ultimately hinder our movement and stunt our growth in our walk with the Lord. These thoughts and feelings will remove any motivation for us to move on, causing us to just want to lie down and accept the mundane without the hope of anything better.

I want to share an illustration that occurred a few years ago while I was spending some time with my grandson Corey. We were fishing at the mouth of a tributary to the Susquehanna River, south of Harrisburg, Pennsylvania. It was an area that had experienced constant flooding during heavy rains, and as a result, a very large log had jammed against the bank but still protruded out into the tributary several feet. I determined that as each storm had occurred and the river rose, more debris would gather around this large log, which was now blocking the flow of the water out into the creek.

Just on the other side of this clutter, fish were jumping up out of the water gathering insects that came near, and every time Corey tried to cast out where the fish were leaping, his line would become stuck in the debris. After several unsuccessful attempts to hook a fish, he eventually grabbed a very large and lengthy branch of wood and began to jab at the pile of clutter that had accumulated there. With each poke of his limb, chunks of debris would dislodge and float away. Then Corey decided to turn his attention to the log itself, which had created the whole mess. With a few more precise jabs and some muscle power, the entire log, along with the debris, eventually broke free and was gone, giving us access to the goal we were after—catching those fish.

This is a picture of what may happen to us in our own life journey. An event occurs that creates a blockage that slows down or stops our progress. We then allow that event and the results of it to remain in place. Another event quickly follows that compounds the present situation, all of it negative, and before you know it, we can't help but to focus on this new overwhelming problem and its consequences, which happen to be blocking the flow of God's Spirit in our lives.

As we continue to experience the setback, depression sets in and despair takes over. There is no strength or willpower left to fight back, and we accept the circumstances, believing it's God's will that we suffer rather than choosing to do something positive to rid ourselves of these obstacles. But may we be reminded that Jesus suffered so that we wouldn't have to. I'm not saying we won't have to go through some tough times and experience some hardships; what I am saying is that God never intended for us to remain there as a permanent dwelling place.

Maybe you're reading this book and finding yourself in such a place as this. If so, you need to do what Corey did. Look around you and find the tools that God has placed nearby—His Word, prayer, and using your faith in His limitless power—and begin to jab at those attitudes or feelings, circumstances, or situations that are piercing your soul. It's here, as you activate the gifts of God in your life, that things will begin to move in a positive direction. You need to look beyond the present circumstances and focus your eyes on the goal and destination that you originally had in mind.

Take time to ask the Lord to freshen the vision He gave you at the beginning of your journey and then be willing to participate in the answer to your prayers. Corey could have prayed for God to move the jamb, but God gave Corey the wisdom and the means to move it himself. Pick yourself up and say, "Enough is enough"—and let's get back on the road again!

I can tell you truthfully, there's *something more* for you than where you are and what you already possess. God has great things in store as you press into His presence and endeavor to help yourself. But you have to want what God has for you badly enough in order to pursue Him and the prize of His high calling. Don't remain stuck and hopeless, settling for less than God's best for you. Break free of the status quo and go for the gold. Set the bar higher and pursue the reward of His high calling and favor upon your life.

There is an old phrase that's used at the gym, "No pain, no gain." This may be a word for you today. You must be willing to do whatever it takes, paying whatever the cost necessary, to lay hold of God's plans and destiny for your future. What Corey and I saw that lay beyond the obstacle in the river was worth the effort on our part to remove what stood in our way. If you could only see a glimpse of what God has waiting for you on the other side of where you are, nothing would be able to stop you from getting there! Don't come up on the short end and go home without a catch.

I often hear people say, "There's got to be something more!" And oh, how true that is. The Bible tells us, though, that without a vision, the people perish (see Proverbs 29:18). If you don't set goals or set your sight on something to invest your efforts in, you will never move from your current position or situation. I see too many good people who lack the desire to press in, or refuse to invest some time and effort, and thereby miss God's blessings.

I remember a song that the late Kim Clement used to sing on his program—"I'm somewhere in the future, and I look much better than I look right now." Get your eyes off your problems and get them on the team who can solve them—God and you! Be willing to be the answer to the prayers you are praying. God is good all the time, and all the time God is good! He has promised to do exceedingly abundantly above all that we can ask or think, so tap into the resources He has made available and find that *something more* that has already been prepared for you.

In some of my recent encounters, I have found that my surroundings or conditions did not start out very positive, but sometimes God creates uncomfortable situations to get us to move in another direction. I love what it says in Romans 8:28: "And we know that all things work together for good to them that love God, to them who are called according to His purpose" (KJV). In almost 50 years of knowing and serving Him, God has never failed to fulfill His Word and His promises to me, and He's not about to fail me now.

In your own circumstances, how hungry are you for a fresh encounter with the Lord? Has life thrown you a curve ball when you were looking for a fast ball? These are the greatest of times—a day when God is moving, revealing the hidden things, exposing us to the higher heights and deeper depths of His Kingdom purposes. Don't be left on the outside looking in. Don't be a spectator but a participator in all that is happening. Read Romans chapter 8 again and activate those promises in your life. You truly are more than a conqueror, so tap into the *something more* that God has waiting with your name on it!

CHAPTER 7

SERVING LEFTOVERS

I know this sounds like a strange title in the middle of this book, but I feel God wants to speak these two particular words, especially into the hearts of those in leadership, just as He did to mine, at a crucial time in my life. What I'm about to share I have experienced from both sides of the fence. As I have mentioned throughout this book, life's experiences have taught me a lot, and continue to do so.

I grew up in a large family. We lived with my father's parents for the first 13 years of my life. I had five brothers and one sister, so that made 11 people living in a small farmhouse on Bear Mountain in Adams County, Pennsylvania. My father worked as a logger, cutting logs and pulpwood for a living, while my grandfather made axe and hammer handles from trees we harvested on the farm. Then he sold them to local hardware stores and individuals to help pay the bills. We weren't able to partake of the finer things that others enjoyed, but we were blessed with the necessities of life and grew a lot of our own crops. There was very little, if anything, that went to waste around the farm, especially food; and many times Grandma and Mom would cook a little extra so there would be food ready to be warmed over for the next meal. I found that the flavor of some foods was enhanced during reheating and tasted even better the second time around.

As I thought about writing this chapter, I also thought about "serving leftovers" in a whole different light. This chapter is one that, as a leader, I believe can help you to avoid some of the pitfalls of an overloaded schedule and overwhelming lifestyle. In my many years of serving the Lord and assisting various leaders, I have seen what the demands of ministry can do to an individual and to those whom they are serving. Personally, I have served in many different levels of pastoral ministry, from youth ministry to associate pastor, to care pastor, and then senior pastor. Much of what I will share in this chapter are personal experiences and events, some of which I wish I could go back and do differently, knowing what I know now.

I have been told over the years that experience is the best teacher, and I tend to believe that to be a fact. I've had some really wonderful mentors over the years who have taught me a lot about ministry and caring for the Body of Christ. Some of what they shared with me were in areas where they fell short in the demands and responsibilities they carried. I'm not re-sharing these to be critical in any way, and I will not be using any names as a reference, for I respect each one of them and appreciate their investment in my own life. I disclose these things to you so that you might be able to avoid some of the pitfalls as well as the pain, heartache, and disappointment that resulted in the lives of others. I'm surely not trying to paint a negative picture regarding pastoral ministry, for these folks have invested their heart and soul into what they do, and there are far more positive and fruitful results than negative.

As a leader, sometimes we put too much pressure on ourselves to be successful and to produce the results that are expected from our position. Sometimes there are many demands and expectations from those we minister to every day. But may we be reminded that every pastor and leader is a real person with real responsibilities that go beyond all they do for the church. Moreover, the lifestyles of today and the pace of life are far more demanding and different than when I was growing up 60-plus years ago on my grandpa's farm. Many days now, it seems like people are moving faster, the demands of life are speeding along at what seems like 100 miles an hour, and we're expected to keep up with it all. It's off to a job, working long hours to fulfill the demands of the church or a company and its employees. And along with a career commitment, there may be special material items each of us long for and might choose to put in the overtime to be able to afford—perhaps things we missed out on growing up as a child. Then there's the demand to keep up with other family and friends who have achieved success in the occupations they have chosen.

As I was growing up as a child, my family always had time to visit with other extended family almost every weekend. We sat together and shared meals and fellowshipped. Family time was a value we held dear. But in today's world, there's barely time to spend with those who live under our own roof, and many times we don't even eat together because of different schedules. Family time has been sacrificed in the pursuit of a successful career and in order to make more money to buy more things.

We are also living in a time when children are growing up without the daily influence of a father, or mother, or both, and are left to fend for themselves with a lack of moral values. Consequently, they turn to drugs, alcohol, and sex to fulfill their inner desires. They have no real identity or direction in life, and many end up out on the streets selling themselves to the highest bidder, or even worse—dead from violence. You can identify them by their hostility, the clothes they wear, the piercings and tattoos, and the company they keep. God help us to reach out to these children and bring them back to a place of reality and restoration!

But, for now, I want to speak to you who are pastors and leaders. We, too, can be pulled in so many directions that we struggle to do anything well. We strive, labor, and end up overcommitting ourselves to fulfill the demands of being a spouse, a parent, a child taking care of an elderly parent, an employee—both leader and coworker, a volunteer, a good neighbor, and on and on. We would never want to disappoint anyone or come up short in our own expectations. But when we overcommit ourselves, something or someone is going to pay the price. In the roles I just mentioned, the people who we care for may become a victim, rather than aided by our busy lifestyles, and all too often, we leave a chasm of unmet and unfulfilled responsibilities, hurting them and hurting ourselves, destroying our relationships and even our lives.

Over the years I've learned what proper alignment should look like in our relationships, and I understand that it takes personal effort and sacrifice to make those relationships work. First and foremost is our relationship with our heavenly Father; Jesus Christ, His Son; and the Holy Spirit. The first Great Commandment He gave us was to love Him with all our heart, mind, and strength, and to have no other gods before Him (see Exodus chapter 20; Mark 12:30). If we don't begin with God, our life will end up chaotic. Everything else will be out of alignment unless the Lord is at the helm and forefront of our lives. He has ordered our days and our steps, and it is to our benefit to get in rhythm with Him. This doesn't mean that we won't have trials and temptations; but it does mean that when they do come, He will take charge of the situation and turns things around in our favor. Our Father God works all things for our good and desires to bless us with all spiritual blessings in Christ Jesus. The Bible tells us in Third John verse 2:

Beloved, I wish above all things that thou mayest prosper and be in health, even as thy soul prospereth (KJV).

The second most important relationship is with our family, our husband, wife, children, parents, and even our neighbors. God has given me, as a husband, the responsibility to care for, nurture, and provide for my household. Take time to read Ephesians chapter 5 and the directives that Paul gave to the husbands and wives about their responsibilities; then ask yourself the question: "Am I fulfilling them according to Scripture?" These responsibilities are actually not that difficult, because God has given us the blueprint for them.

The third area of responsibility is that of our career or where we earn the means to provide for our families. Any type of employment or job will demand personal dependability and faithfulness to those whom you work for, as well as giving them your best effort to fulfill the expectations of the position you have been entrusted with. This duty could be very demanding according to the level of leadership you hold. The problems begin to arise when we get out of alignment and overcommit to an area that should not take priority over God or family. All too often, our relationship with the Lord, the most important of all, is the one that is sacrificed.

I want to speak especially to you who are in ministry—pastors and associates, evangelists, and department leaders. As pastors, especially with large congregations, and who have no associates to assist you, you can easily be overwhelmed with the demands of ministry. Often, many people expect that God has placed you there to meet all their needs and fix all their problems—spiritual and otherwise. And when you extend the hours each day trying to meet their needs, you have nothing left on your schedule to give to the Lord or your own family. But if you're that busy, then you're too busy. Adjustments need to be made immediately and before a disaster occurs. It's time to raise up others in the church who can assist in carrying out the duties of visitation and ministering to the needs of the people.

If you're not a good steward of your time overall and in every specific area, many people, if not everyone around you, will suffer from your failures. By the time you get to Sunday morning to preach the Word of God, all that will be left to offer the congregation will be what's "left over." If you find yourself in this position, take time out and assess the situation and make the necessary adjustments to get back on the right course. God never meant for the ministry He gave you to destroy you. These things happen when we make bad choices and try to do too much on our own.

Be determined now to make those decisions needed to lighten up on areas of commitment and to even eliminate other areas all together. This task can be very difficult, especially when this type of lifestyle has been deeply engrained within you; but it will ultimately be to your benefit and to the benefit of those you have responsibilities to. God still has great plans and expectations for you as you follow His leading. This is your time to access God's best and to live in the *above and beyond* of His provision!

CHAPTER 8

IT'S TIME TO AWAKEN

Just in my lifetime, I've seen the church become a victim of the culture of this world and have likewise witnessed the spirit of the age infiltrating the church, causing a spiritual slumber to overcome the people of God. Often, the church has given in to the demands of the outside world with the hope that the world will still like or appreciate them. Many of the things that the Bible calls sin are being approved, grieving the heart of God, and the church, as a whole, has become apostate.

In the Book of Acts, when the Church was birthed, it was birthed and bathed in the power and authority of the Holy Spirit (see Acts 2:1-4). It was called to go into all the world and transform the lives of people and nations, by delivering them from a worldly system of darkness and degradation, and by bringing forth the Kingdom of God in holiness and righteousness. God gave the people of the Church the power to perform signs, wonders, and miracles wherever they went and to bring order where there was anarchy. Souls were saved, bodies were healed, those bound by satanic powers were loosed and set free, and the needs of the people were met by the supernatural power of God. I wonder, how many churches are you aware of today that still operate in these same areas?

You see, the Holy Spirit came into the upper room to accomplish and fulfill the promise of God, but He didn't remain there; and neither did those who were filled. He took up residence within those who received Him, the one hundred and twenty, and wherever they went, His power flowed out of them and touched lives in miraculous ways. As a result, thousands were saved daily!

Today, God is likewise looking for people who will tarry in His presence until they are filled with His power, who will hearken to His voice and obey the call and commission to reach out to a lost and hurting generation (see Matthew 28:18-20). But we, as the modern-day church, have set our own agendas, and we do "church" the way we think it should be done, or according to the traditions set by our forefathers. Consequently, many people never see the supernatural power of God at work in our midst. All too often, church is managed like a business and is programmed by man so that there's no opportunity for the Holy Spirit to move. We want church to be convenient and compatible to our schedules rather than make a personal sacrifice that could possibly bring a major breakthrough in our lives.

Yet, even now, there is a fresh stirring that is taking place, and I believe it's out of a desperation from the people for another "great awakening" that will begin to restore the Church upon the foundations recorded in the Book of Acts. We must come to the place where we're sick and tired of dead, dry services that are filled with empty words and no results, where people leave the sanctuary pretty much the way they came in. God wants to breathe new life as well as a fresh fire of the Holy Spirit into His Bride!

In reading the testimonies and accounts of those who were part of the prior awakenings that have taken place, we learn that the people had to first come to a place of hunger and desperation, where they gathered and prayed, many for hours on end, and sacrificed meals and schedules while waiting on the Lord. They came with repentant hearts, asking the Lord to forgive them and were willing to turn from their wicked ways to serve the Lord. The Word of God once again became a priority and was read, and prayed with compassion, and proclaimed as the truth that the people would stand upon.

The Scriptures tell us that when we stray from the Lord, there is a way back to Him, a way to reenter into a right standing with our heavenly Father. In Second Chronicles 7:12b and 14, we read that the Lord appeared to Solomon by night and said to him:

I have heard thy prayer, and have chosen this place to Myself for an house of sacrifice. If I shut up heaven that there be no rain, or if I command the locusts to devour the land, or if I send pestilence among My people; if My people, which are called by My name, shall humble themselves, and pray, and turn from their wicked ways; then will I hear from heaven, and will forgive their sin, and will heal their land (KJV).

Here we see the process of restoration as spoken by God, and it still works today! I so long to see the Church, as a whole, and not just the one I worship in, raised up, restored, and operating in God's power and authority so that the lives of multitudes will be transformed and then empowered to touch others with the same anointing of the Holy Spirit.

Yet we have drifted away from many of the core values of the early Church and fallen prey to the spirit of this age and the modern-day culture. Our desire for success and obtaining more things has taken us away from the true source of happiness and fulfillment. Remember, only Jesus can satisfy and fill the void within. As I shared earlier, much of what the Bible says is very clear about as being sin, now is being accepted as a way of life. The approval from men is desired above God's commands to be holy as He is holy. This desire has already begun to bring judgment upon this nation and shut off the flow of the Holy Spirit within the church. God cannot pour His Holy Spirit into an unclean vessel.

One term we have heard so much of during the past 20 years is being "politically correct." I liken it to a slow form of death, like a cancer eating away at the body until all that's left is a valley of dead, dry bones (see Ezekiel 37:1-10). For the most part, those in leadership and a few within the Church have realized what has actually been happening during this period of time. Yet many people believe that God will understand, for He knows the pressure we're under, and even though it's not what He has willed for us, He'll be gracious. That, my friend, is presuming upon the grace of God, and that is a dangerous place to be. God sets the standard high for a purpose, and when we operate below that level, we cancel out His Word over us and lose our testimony before those we're trying to win into the Kingdom.

So let me ask you, what's it going to take to see another great awakening here in the Church in America? I believe it must start within you and me, and involve a shift in our priorities and desires. Yet, many often sit back and wait, expecting that a special individual will come along, preach a series of messages under the power of the Holy Spirit, and ignite a fire within those of the church...or something like that will happen to start the ball rolling. It very well could happen, but in times past, an awakening started with those present joining together, declaring a season of prayer and fasting, and repenting and calling on the name of the Lord to come and restore, refresh, and renew their relationship with Him. There aren't many superstars in God's Kingdom, only those who have given their all so that they can receive His all!

The fact is, what we need, or should I say, Who we need, is already here. He's been here, and now He resides within us—the Holy Spirit. Revival lives within—the power to overcome lives within. May our cry be for Him to fill us until we overflow with God's power and love! Everything we need is already available. For way too long we've taken a soft approach to partnering with the Lord to propagate an awakening. Now, much of the desperation we feel is a result of the current events in the world, which should drive us to our knees and begin to pray, seek His face, and ignite the fires.

If we will take time out from all our other activities, turn off the TV, and shut down the computers and Facebook accounts long enough to hear what God has to say to us, He will give us the strategies to spark another great awakening right where we are. We're not waiting on God. God is waiting on us.

Many of the same issues of today also existed back in Solomon's time. People are no longer looking to the Lord but at their own situations. They have begun to worship other gods and have drifted into complacency and apathy, questioning the true existence of God while indulging in sinful pleasures. Consequently, God can only lift His hand of blessing and protection off of such a people who ignore and forsake Him. And it's a dangerous place to find one's self.

Yet, there's still time for us to call on the Lord. He is looking for a Daniel or a Nehemiah who will stand in the gap and repent on behalf of a rebellious people and their leaders. Although some people say that it's too late for America and that we've gone too far, I dare to differ. While the window of opportunity is closing, and time is of the essence, the Church still can awaken from its slumbering state and make a stand, repent and turn from her wicked ways, and walk in obedience to and in alignment with His Word and His will, so that revival comes to America once again.

At the time of this writing, I have joined with several groups of pastors and leaders who have brought their churches and congregations together, and we have begun to pray. We've put aside denominational barriers and are standing in the gap for our region and this nation. As a result, there has been an increase of salvations and healings, transformation is happening within our communities, and God is exposing evil alliances and beginning to dismantle strongholds. Let's keep the momentum going and spread the word. Gather those around you and begin to pray together regularly until God moves.

It's time we contend for the things deemed important to the Kingdom of God. Let's put aside any personal distraction and agendas and spend more time asking God for His wisdom, revelation, and direction regarding how to move forward and how to carry out His will in the earth. May the Lord awaken you so that you become a catalyst in birthing the next great awakening in America!

I want to conclude this chapter with the words of Paul in his letter to the church at Ephesus.

Wherefore I also, after I heard of your faith in the Lord Jesus, and love unto all the saints, cease not to give thanks for you, making mention of you in my prayers; that the God of our Lord Jesus Christ, the Father of glory, may give unto you the spirit of wisdom and revelation in the knowledge of Him: the eyes of your understanding being enlightened; that ye may know what is the hope of His calling, and what the riches of the glory of His inheritance in the saints, and what is the exceeding greatness of His power to us-ward who believe, according to the working of His mighty power, which He wrought in Christ, when He raised Him from the dead, and set Him at His own right hand in the heavenly places, far above all principality, and power, and might, and dominion, and every name that is named, not only in this world, but also in that which is to come: and hath put all things under His feet, and gave Him to be the head over all things to the church, which is His body, the fulness of Him that filleth all in all (Ephesians 1:15-23 KJV)

Godspeed to each of you as you follow His lead.

CHAPTER 9

FROM AWAKENING TO SOARING—NO LONGER EARTHBOUND

I've always been amazed by and attracted to eagles. Interestingly, we have recently seen eagles flying around our home. These birds are very unique in how they live and move about. They are not only our national bird, but they are also found in Scripture on many occasions. In this chapter, I want to encourage you to begin to move to new levels, as that of an eagle, to a higher calling that God has for you. Moreover, realizing that God has so much more ahead, should be entice and propel you to progress into and fulfill His will and purpose.

I'm tired of hearing people say they've been saved for so many years when it's obvious they have never grown and matured past their salvation experience. I call these individuals "earthbound Christians"—with only one goal in mind—and that is to get to Heaven. There's definitely nothing wrong with that goal, but between their initial salvation experience and promotion to glory, there's a whole lot of living to be done.

God's Great Commission isn't just to see people converted, but also to make disciples, so that they in turn can mature in their walk with the Lord and minister to others. It's sad to see so many people live lives of wasted years with no goals or incentives to venture above and beyond such an immature level of relationship with the Lord and His Church. These usually become high-maintenance people who often need extra special care and attention.

So many times when I ask people if they know the Lord, their reply is something like, "I go to church," or "I call myself a Christian," or "I know the Lord." Going to church does not make you a Christian, and believing there is a God doesn't fully suffice either.

Even the devil and his demons believe there is a God. The proof of truly knowing Him is by having a born-again encounter with the Lord, that which leads to a personal relationship, a transformed life, and a change of direction in how we live and walk every day.

The devil has done a good job of robbing people of their true identity, thus limiting their ability to mature into their God-given call in life. But on the other hand, we are also living in a time when people are finding out who they are, by making good decisions to walk in obedience to the Lord, and then allowing the work of His Holy Spirit to operate in their lives.

Getting back to the eagle, some of the character traits of the eagle are those that God desires for us, His spiritual eagles, His sons and daughters, to display as we navigate through a world where there are many challenges that confront us daily. Let's take some time to look at this majestic bird and see how we can be equipped to not only face those obstacles but to triumph over them and grow stronger in the process.

Of all the birds of the earth, the eagle is the most graceful yet powerful. He is utterly fearless in the very face of adversity and possesses the ability to soar above the turmoil, the confusion, and the challenges, rising into a realm of peace far beyond. When thinking about the analogy of eagles in Scripture, the first verse that comes to mind is Isaiah 40:31:

> *But they that wait upon the Lord shall renew their strength; they shall mount up with wings as eagles; they shall run, and not be weary; and they shall walk, and not faint* (KJV).

The eagle here is a symbol of an overcoming Christian who can stand with boldness and endurance in the face of adversity and not be overwhelmed or overcome by what he sees or feels in the natural. Christians are moved upon and empowered by the Word of God and the power of the Holy Spirit.

The Hebrew word for "wait" is *qavah*, which means "to bind together as by twisting." It's like weaving strands of several cords together to form a rope. Alone, a single cord is limited in strength, but intertwined with another, its strength and capability multiplies. To "mount up" means to rise up to new levels, to soar to new heights that will carry us above and beyond all the former limitations we faced. The Bible tells us in John 16:33b, "In the world ye shall have tribulation: but be of good cheer; I have overcome the world" (KJV). It's in these times of adversity that God proves faithful and true to us, for it is then that He provides all that we need to overcome the circumstances and to defeat our enemies. It's then we can have peace and rest in the midst of life's trials and tests.

One of the strengths of the eagle is that it has learned how to use the turbulence, the winds of adversity, to its benefit. Of all the eagles I've noticed, I've never seen one continually flapping its wings or struggling to stay in flight. The eagle knows how to spread its wings and use the power in the thermal updrafts of winds to lift itself higher. (Many times in the lower elevations, smaller birds tend to harass the eagle, but as the eagle rises up and soars higher, the smaller birds are unable to follow him. Sounds like a good plan to me!) These thermal updrafts make it almost effortless for the eagle to not only fly, but to soar to great altitudes. Some ascend so high that the naked eye can no longer see them. In addition, they can reach speeds in excess of 80 miles per hour. The very conditions that you think in the natural would work against their flight are actually the aspects that launch them to new altitudes!

Another asset the eagle possesses is excellent vision. The higher the eagle flies, the larger the field of vision becomes, helping it to detect its prey. The eagle's vision is believed to be five times greater than man's, enabling it to locate snakes, mice, and other food sources. It's not difficult to see why God uses the eagle as an example of what He desires to see in His spiritual sons and daughters. He wants to teach us how to catch the wind of the Holy Spirit and then soar to new heights with increased vision.

The higher we soar in the Spirit, the more we can observe trouble afar off and then be able to avoid the dangers that would ensnare us and cause us to crash to the earth. Eagle Christians can learn to soar without effort by catching the thermal winds of the Holy Spirit. In the Scriptures, there are also references to the "wind of God" or the "breath of God." The Hebrew word used is *ruach*. When we are "born again," God breathes His breath of new life into us; consequently, we become dead to the old man and are made alive in Christ. His *ruach* is our life-giving source! God never meant for us to dwell continually in the valley of despair and defeat, but to be seated in "heavenly places" in Christ Jesus (see Ephesians 2:6 KJV). It is a real place, a position in the spirit realm where the things that once troubled us and caused us to walk in fear, keeping us earthbound, are now beneath us, under our feet.

Far too many Christians, though, have never learned to rise to new heights in the Lord; instead, they have allowed their circumstances to keep them ensnared where they can no longer spread their wings and fly. Some have even come up with the idea that remaining in their circumstances helps keep them humble and submissive. Give me a break! They end up going through the motions of singing, praying, and giving, yet they never experience the blessings of the Lord and soaring to the higher heights God meant for them to have.

Much of this can be the result of remaining under their current leadership, leaders who, themselves, have never learned how to rise above the standard of earthly birds. You can bring people only to the same level you operate out of. Some other reasons for "staying grounded" may involve the training that Christians have received when they were younger, or it may be the fear of stepping into unchartered territory or the fear of failure. God help us as leaders to never be the reason that deprives others of the greater blessings God has made available.

Don't let present or past circumstances hold you back from the great things God has destined for you. Don't let the actions of under-achievers deprive and rob you. Don't let them talk you out of the adventures that await you. And don't allow the deceiver to abort your destiny. God has a divine call upon your life!

One of the main tormentors of the eagle is the crow. This bird will constantly plague any lone eagle, or young eagles, and fly next to them in order to taunt them. They are the dirty birds that make a lot of noise and aggravate the others around them. I wonder if you have ever met one of these "birds." In the church realm, they are the gossipers, people who very seldom have anything good to say about anybody or anything. They continually criticize others, especially those who have risen to new levels in their walk with the Lord, far beyond where they themselves have ventured to go. They also may be people who find it easier to pull others down to their level, rather than put forth the effort to rise up and soar with "wings as eagles." Be very careful about whom you associate with, and do what is necessary to prevent yourself from becoming their prey or allowing them to victimize your flight plans.

Our main goal in life should be to fellowship with our heavenly Father and live in the fullness of His presence, to fulfill His Word and will in our lives by using every asset He has provided us with, and to touch the lives of the multitudes we meet each and every day. May we help others to encounter God and begin to soar with Him, with "wings as eagles." If there is to be another "great awakening" and if there is any hope of restoring this nation back to its God-given purpose, it must start with you and me. We are the blood-bought Church of Jesus Christ, and we must rise up in the power and authority that God has commissioned to us, by thus allowing the Holy Spirit to lead and use us.

There are new territories to explore, more enemies to conquer, and new lands to possess; but it will not be accomplished by being religious or complacent. It does not mean joining a church, although that is a good thing, but it will happen when we pray as Jesus prayed in the Garden of Gethsemane: "Father..., not My will but Yours be done (see Matthew 26:39 NIV)."

Zechariah 4:6 says it well:

Then he answered and spake unto me, saying, This is the word of the Lord unto Zerubbabel, saying, Not by might, nor by power, but by My Spirit, saith the Lord of hosts (KJV).

We expend so much time, energy, and resources in programs and events that end up in frustration and fruitlessness, when truly, what we need to do is pray for the wisdom of the Lord and a move of the Holy Spirit. On the Day of Pentecost, God took 120 ordinary people, filled them with His power, and launched the greatest revival ever seen in that day. People were saved by the thousands, bodies were healed, and those possessed by demons were set free. And the Church grew "daily"!

The question is, are you ready—are you hungry and thirsty, for a fresh move of the Holy Spirit in your life? Are you tired of the spiritual crows pecking at you and bringing discouragement and defeat? Are you ready to acquire your eagle's wings and begin to soar to new heights and become one of God's mature eagles, those He is raising up this very hour who will help usher in this next move of God?

His provision for you is readily available, and He awaits your request to get on board. Time is of the essence, and souls are hanging in the balance. It's time for God's eagle army to rise up, catch the thermal winds, and soar! Go for it!

CHAPTER 10

ABOVE OUR UNDERSTANDING

We live in a day and time when knowledge is increasing every moment. As a result, new inventions, which ease the labor from our lives, are developed every day—even cars that drive themselves. I grew up when you had to get off the couch in order change the channels on a black-and-white TV, but now, everyone uses a clicker to access several hundred channels provided by satellites floating around in space.

Computers are our modern communication devices that provide access to all kinds of knowledge by just entering a name, or place, or subject. Nowadays, it takes very little research or human effort to tap into a wealth of data. There are times I wish I had had that kind of technology available when I was young. And consider our cell phones that do so much more than make phone calls. They call them "smart phones," for there's not much they can't do. They are literally pocket computers that can be used to reach the other side of the world and include a built-in GPS system to show you how to get there.

Even with all this wealth of knowledge and ability to communicate, I want to write this chapter, looking at knowledge from a spiritual perspective and as it pertains to our personal relationship with our heavenly Father. For we have been created in His likeness and image, created to have fellowship with the Father, Son, and Holy Spirit (see Genesis 1:26-28 KJV).

In the beginning, God gave man authority and dominion over all the other areas of creation—the land, the animals, the birds, and life in the sea. To rule over this creation, Adam needed an awareness and knowledge of each of these things, the wisdom to co-habitat with them, and to learn how they could reproduce. God likewise gave Adam the privilege of naming every one of those things.

We also know, that in the midst of all this, God placed two trees in the Garden of Eden—the tree of life, of which Adam and Eve could partake, and the tree of the knowledge of good and evil, of which they were forbidden to eat. There was also a serpent, a fallen cherub named satan, who roamed the Garden. One day, at an opportune time while Eve was alone, satan devised and enacted a plan of deception, to destroy the first couple's intimate relationship with Father God and have them banned from the Garden. John 10:10 tells us that "The thief cometh not, but for to steal, and to kill, and to destroy…" (KJV). And he's still at it today.

Satan proceeded by creating doubt in Eve's mind and convincing her that God was holding out secret things from her and Adam, by not allowing them to partake of the fruit of the tree of the knowledge of good and evil. What both Adam and Eve failed to realize was that they were already like God in every way, perfect and sinless. But because satan sowed a seed of doubt in their minds, they questioned God's authority and guidelines; and to see if there might be something more that would establish them on a level equal with their heavenly Father, they developed a desire for the fruit. Adam and Eve gave into the temptation and sinned against God, disobeying His command to not eat of this particular tree. This disobedience is the very thing that got satan booted out of Heaven.

Knowledge continues to be an area today where mankind challenges himself to keep searching what is presently unknown while constantly developing new things, new ideas, and new ways of living life—striving to return to the way it might have been in that perfect environment in the Garden. Let's consider again what I shared as I began this chapter—look how far man's knowledge has advanced in the past 50 years and how rapidly it's changing almost daily. It makes you wonder where it will take us in the future, even within our own lifetime.

It reminds me of the story in the Bible about the Tower of Babel (see Genesis chapter 11). The people decided to build this tower into the heavenlies in order to reach the dwelling place of God. Consequently, God brought confusion upon them, and the people began to speak different languages, which broke their ability to communicate as well as to build. What "knowledge" might we ourselves be pressing toward that will be thwarted by the hand of God? I believe one of the next great events, along with a great awakening and the harvest of souls, will be the coming of the Lord. It is my personal view that the world cannot continue on this pace without divine intervention.

Now, returning to my main focal point of this chapter—knowledge and understanding. The realm of the spirit, God's realm, has remained a mystery for the most part, although God has been unveiling things piece by piece to those who have pressed into a deeper level of intimacy with Him. He desires to share much of what is unknown to man in these last days, knowledge that will bring a greater understanding of the times and seasons we are entering.

I believe that greater revelation will soon be released and God will open up the spirit realm that will empower His remnant Bride to perform great miracles, signs, and wonders—which will astound even the wise. At present, we need a great awakening to cause the Church, His Bride, to come to that place of impartation. All this will lead to the greatest harvest of souls the world has ever seen.

When God created Adam and Eve, He did give to them great knowledge and understanding, but yet He didn't impart total and complete understanding, which belonged only to the Godhead. The Scriptures tell us that now we see in part and know in part, but one day we will see clearly and completely. Line upon line and precept upon precept, God is opening up revelation knowledge so that we can be partakers of that knowledge and understanding. What an exciting time to be alive and serving the Lord!

Down through the corridors of time, there have been those who have tapped into this reservoir of knowledge and understanding, beholding outbreaks of signs, wonders, and miracles. These were periods of time, some months and others years in length, that we call revivals or awakenings. In my heart I believe that we should be living at that level of relationship with the Lord every day, rather than simply watch it come and go. Unfortunately, man has caused its departure by putting his hands and human knowledge on something that only God can orchestrate.

But, even now, as the end of this age draws near, I am sensing a hunger in the Body of Christ, His Church, a desperation to press into His presence once again and receive a new level and dimension of wisdom and understanding, well beyond any place we've ever been. As this happens, many of those things that were hidden and remained a mystery will become present knowledge and understanding, and God will use it to bring breakthroughs. God will perform the supernatural and cause many to shake their heads in disbelief, saying, "We've never seen anything like this before." It will touch the multitudes and transform regions for the glory of God with the advancement of His Kingdom on the earth.

As we look at the present world condition, we need to understand that it will only get worse. The Lord has warned us that in these last days, evil will increase, and perilous times will come (see 2 Timothy 3:1 KJV). But in the midst of all the turmoil and strife, God will release an anointing of His Holy Spirit upon His people that will be a yoke-breaking, sin-destroying, eye-opening event, which will bring many to a saving knowledge of the Lord. It's called Harvestime! Satan will once again try to create a spirit of deception and attempt to duplicate God's supernatural power of miracles, signs, and wonders; but only our God is all-powerful, and the true will be separated from the false. The devil's time is short, and knowing this, he is pulling out all the stops to deceive and destroy lives. But God has given us a spirit of discernment to know the real from the fake and to use the tools to accomplish the work He has for you to do.

This is where you and I come upon the scene. As we get more desperate and hungry for the fullness of the Holy Spirit, as we re-dedicate ourselves to prayer and fasting and seeking the Lord, as well as spending more time reading and studying His Word, God will release mantles of ministry so that we can operate in a greater level of wisdom and understanding. Even though we should never underestimate His power and willingness to use us, even some of the things that we will see God do, will astound us. We will stand in awe of His great power and His love for fallen man. It's time to fulfill the "Great Commission" here on the earth. God is waiting for you and me to make that step of commitment and to press into His presence. Believe me when I say, it will be *far above our present understanding and will take us far beyond our greatest expectations.* Remember, the best is yet to come!

CHAPTER 11

BEYOND OUR EXPECTATIONS

Perhaps you are a little like me—you like to dream or envision about what life could be like if … if you had more money, if you had lived in a different location, if you had a better job, or if you could get connected to the right people who could equip you to fulfill all these dreams. Our lives are often filled with unmet expectations. So, in this final chapter, I'd like to take a few moments and relive some of my personal history and adventures regarding dreams and expectations, even those that ended up beyond my expectations.

I was born on July 4, 1949, in Gettysburg, Pennsylvania, and almost immediately received the nickname "Firecracker" because fireworks were exploding in the park next to the hospital when I was born. At the age of six months, I returned to the hospital but was sent home to die from pneumonia. God healed me, though, through the prayers of family and church, even though we were not what you would have called a religious family.

As I previously mentioned, I grew up in a home with five brothers and one sister, where I was the oldest. We lived with my father's parents on their farm until 1962. Four other brothers were born with muscular dystrophy, and all died very young. Because of the hardships, my father turned to alcohol as a sedative, and due to the destruction it caused in his body, he died at the age of 47.

I began to work for a neighbor on his fruit farm at the age of eight, and from that time on, work became a major part of my life. Because of my family's financial and social status, I was made fun of and endured a lot of verbal abuse while growing up. (It was probably good that I wasn't a fighter or I might be doing prison ministry from within the walls.) Naturally, as a young boy, I had expectations of living a different type of life than what I was presently experiencing. I had always loved baseball and thought about growing up to be a professional player, but that dream soon was lost in high school when I could not even make the team.

At the age of 17, and during the time I was a senior in high school, a gentleman who my father worked for began to invite me to attend Gettysburg Foursquare Gospel Church with him. Previously, I had grown up attending a local Methodist church near my home, but after visiting this new church, I realized what a difference there was in how church was done. I had never been in a Pentecostal church before, and what I saw and experienced, including how people expressed their love for the Lord and His presence, was quite a shock to me. After a few months of attending, the Holy Spirit brought conviction upon me one Sunday morning at the end of Pastor Myers' message, and I made my way to the altar and accepted the Lord into my heart. That's when I began to experience what real life was all about!

Shortly thereafter, I became involved in the youth group, and the youth pastor, Ron Myers, started to give me responsibilities during the meetings. You have to understand something here—after all the verbal abuse I went through earlier in my life, I had withdrawn myself and was scared to death of standing in front of people for fear of more abuse. Little did I know at the time that God was preparing me for a journey into fulltime ministry many years down the road.

During this time, I also began to date the most beautiful blonde-haired young lady. Her name was Wanda McGlaughlin, and as of this writing, she has been my wife for 47 years. I had often thought that no woman would ever want anyone like me with my background, but God, once again, had other plans. I can truly say that I married up in class on our wedding day in February of 1970.

Together we remained involved in the youth ministry, and when the youth pastor left for the mission field, Wanda and I served as youth leaders for about two years until a new youth pastor arrived. Also during this time in youth ministry, I began to lead worship and eventually led worship in the main services. Then in 1976, Wanda and I left the Foursquare Church to help a friend, Pastor Joe Fissel, pioneer Heritage Assembly of God Church in Gettysburg. Pastor Fissel also eventually formed a quartet, and we traveled on Sunday nights, singing, preaching, and sharing about the new church as well as gaining financial support from other Assembly churches.

In 1978, I was laid off from my job with the Pennsylvania Department of Transportation after a career of ten years and then took another job working for the construction company that was building our new church. I continued to travel and work for them for the next eight years. Meanwhile, in 1980, I also began to travel and sing and minister on my own; and we were led by God to become part of Bethel Assembly of God in Littlestown, Pennsylvania where we would be involved in several areas of ministry. Wanda and I also traveled over a five-state area for the next 12 years. As for my secular job, in 1985, I accepted another position for a large builder in Columbia, Maryland as a service manager. My duties there dealt with problems and repairs needed by homeowners and coordinating the necessary work with subcontractors and my own employees.

Without going into a lot of detail, I approached a season of change and transition in 1997, which led me to take a deep personal look with regard to my relationship with the Lord and subsequently making a renewed commitment of my life to Him. I call it my "all in" season. Consequently, I resigned my position with the builder in Columbia and sought the Lord for His new direction. Some 18 months later, I was hired at Bethel by my Senior Pastor James Ruddy as his Prayer and Care Pastor, once again dealing with people's problems and issues. It's funny how the previous job prepared me for my next assignment. As I've mentioned at various times throughout this book, God is always one step ahead of us.

During this particular transition, the Lord connected us with key people, such as LaNora Morin in Phoenix, Arizona and Chuck Pierce in Denton, Texas, which He used to speak prophetically into our lives. New doors began to open, and a new level of God's anointing poured into our lives. In the meantime, we began Intercessory Prayer meetings in the church every week, praying for a move of God over our church and our region. The Holy Spirit flooded our meetings with His presence, and the church exploded. We added Friday night "River Services" to our regular schedule, and God continued to bless us. There's too much to share of what happened, much of what could be used to write another book. Suffice it to say that the church grew numerically as well as spiritually, and we went into a large building program. During this time, God invested more and more into our lives, and there were those times when I felt like I had arrived at my destiny in the Lord—yet God had something more.

In 2013, my Senior Pastor James Ruddy accepted a new position in Buffalo, New York, and I was asked to temporarily fill the senior pastor position. It was a battle I fought for several weeks, feeling insufficient for the role, but God assured me that He was large and in charge, and all would be well. Once again, these circumstances went beyond my expectations. Even during this time of transition, God was connecting us with key people who would have a part in what was yet to come.

I want to take a moment here and add a few thoughts that may help you where you are at in your own circumstances and what you are going through. One of the areas of ministry that was vital and helpful during these transitions was the prophetic ministry. God connected us to several individuals who operated in a very strong and accurate level of prophecy, and the Lord spoke through them, confirming His direction for us, step by step.

I know that a lot of pastors and leaders get nervous when we talk about prophetic ministry, primarily because it has been misused and abused by many for personal gain. Even so, it is extremely valuable and important to the advancement of what God is doing in this hour. I know there have been negative issues, but don't throw the ministry away because of a few who have taken personal advantage of it. May God give you the discernment to know the real from the fake.

At this point, it may seem like a long, drawn-out story, so let me wrap it up for you. In January 2015, I was released from my pastoral duties at Bethel, and a new journey began, a season of transition. The wonderful part of all of this is that even though I wasn't prepared to go through another change, God already had a plan in place and was working on it during my last few months there. I have learned a lot of valuable lessons over the years of change, some the hard way because I was stubborn and didn't want to move on. Change for the most part is never easy, but often necessary.

During an evening of intercessory prayer, God gave me the name for the ministry He was now calling Wanda and me to—Above and Beyond Ministries. This ministry will be used to help pastors and leaders who are struggling to arise to new heights and fulfill their God-given call. I'm not here to say I have it all figured out and we have arrived as experts. What I am able to offer is what God has done for us and share with others all that He has given to us, so that they might be able to avoid some of the hard things we went through on the way here.

. Making a personal decision to be "all in" is the first step. Then to spend quality time in God's presence on a daily basis is the next. In those times, He will speak to you directly and download your assignments for each new day. You can't give out to others what you haven't received yourself. I know relationships are important, but even so, don't depend solely on someone else to speak into your life. Rather, allow the Lord that privilege as often as possible.

Maybe you have been wounded by another brother or sister in the Lord, or maybe you have felt the pains of rejection in the past. Whatever these wounds are, choose to forgive those who have hurt or disappointed you, and move on. If you've given up and become discouraged, get back on your feet, get in your prayer closet, and get reinstated and rejuvenated! God is far from finished with you. I could have quit at any point in my journey, but I chose not to. I want to encourage you to do likewise and stay the course.

God is faithful, and the work that He has begun in you He will bring to completion if you don't quit and give up. What lies ahead for you is far greater than what is behind. Take to heart the words of the apostle Paul and the mind-set he carried in Philippians 3:12-14:

Not as though I had already attained, either were already perfect; but I follow after, if that I may apprehend that for which also I am apprehended of Christ Jesus. Brethren, I count not myself to have apprehended: but this one thing I do, forgetting those things which are behind, reaching forth unto those things which are before, I press toward the mark for the prize of the high calling of God in Christ Jesus (KJV).

That really sums it all up in a few verses. God is the Author and Finisher of our faith, and He that has begun a good work in you will be faithful to complete it! (See also Hebrews 12:2; Philippians 1:6 KJV.) Pastors and leaders, brothers and sisters in the Lord, don't allow anything to hinder or stop you from being all that God has called and destined you to be. Don't miss out on what's ahead. Instead, get ready to be released from the Throne Room of Heaven. God is awakening His Bride. There is a stirring in the atmosphere—a call from Heaven is resounding. Open your ears to hear the roar of the Lion of Judah! Hear what He is saying to you personally and respond to Him by saying, "Speak, Lord, for Your servant is listening. Here I am. Use me, Lord. Fill me, and send me where You desire!"

What God has already begun to do is *far above our understanding and far beyond our expectations*! So quit trying to figure it out, quit offering excuses as to why you can't change or move, and get on board and do it!

May the days ahead be filled with all His goodness and glory, and may the Lord exceed all your hopes, dreams, and expectations. In Jesus' name, Amen!

Garry and his wife Wanda founded Above & Beyond Ministries in 2016. Together, they have a deep passion for the Presence of God and seek to stir the same in others with the purpose of leading people into a deeper relationship with the Lord Jesus Christ. They possess an excitement and expectancy of reaching above and going beyond human boundaries to see people fulfill their God-given destinies.

You can connect with them here:

www.bestisyettocome.org
twitter: @_Above_Beyond

Powered by eGenco

Generation Culture Transformation
Specializing in publishing for generation culture change

Visit us Online at:
www.micro65.com

Write to: eGenco
824 Tallow Hill Road
Chambersburg, PA 17202, USA
Phone: 717-461-3436
Email: info@micro65.com

facebook.com/egenbooks
youtube.com/egenpub
egen.co/blog
pinterest.com/eGenDMP
twitter.com/eGenDMP
instagram.com/egenco_dmp